Soaring Eagles

Charlotte Guillain

Chicago, Illinois

Edited by Daniel Nunn, Rebecca Rissman,
and Catherine Veitch
Designed by Victoria Allen
Picture research by Mica Brancic
Production by Victoria Fitzgerald
Originated by Capstone Global Library Ltd
Printed and bound in China by CTPS

17 16 15 14 13
10 9 8 7 6 5 4 3 2 1

Library of Congress Cataloging-in-Publication Data
Guillain, Charlotte.
  Soaring eagles / Charlotte Guillain.
     pages cm.—(Walk on the wild side)
  Includes bibliographical references and index.
  ISBN 978-1-4109-5220-2 (hb)—ISBN 978-1-4109-5227-
1 (pb) 1. Eagles—Juvenile literature. I. Title.
  QL696.F32G854 2013
  598.9'42—dc23   2012034702

Acknowledgments
We would like to thank the following for permission to
reproduce photographs: Corbis pp. 14 (Reuters/Shamil
Zhumatov); FLPA pp. 21 (David Tipling), 23 (Harri
Taavetti), 27 (Michael Callan); Getty Images pp. 9 (Oxford
Scientific/Gavin Parsons), 17 (National Geographic/Klaus
Nigge); Nature Picture Library pp. 4 (© Matthew Maran),
5 (© Edwin Giesbers), 7 (© Roy Mangersnes), 10 (©
Pete Cairns), 11 (© Hanne & Jens Eriksen), 13© David
Tipling, 15 (© Roy Mangersnes), 16 (© Tony Heald), 18
(© Pete Cairns), 20 (© Angelo Gandolfi), 24 (© Grzegorz
Lesniewski), 25 (© Louis Gagnon), 26 (© Wild Wonders
of Europe/Shpilenok), 28 (© Luis Quinta), 29 (© Markus
Varesvuo); Photoshot p. 22 (© NHPA/Jaanus Jarva);
Shutterstock pp. 8 (janbugno), 12 (© Paul van den Berg),
19 (© Rihardzz).

Cover photograph of an American Bald Eagle reproduced
with permission of Getty Images (Rolf Hicker).

We would like to thank Michael Bright for his invaluable
help in the preparation of this book.

Every effort has been made to contact copyright holders
of material reproduced in this book. Any omissions will
be rectified in subsequent printings if notice is given to
the publisher.

Some words are shown in bold, **like this**. You can find
out what they mean by looking in the glossary.

Contents

Introducing Eagles .4

Where Do Eagles Live? 6

What Do Eagles Look Like? 8

Wings and Tails 10

Beaks and Talons. 12

Hunting 14

Different Skills 16

Excellent Eyesight 18

Diving 20

Partners 22

Aeries 24

Eggs and Eaglets. 26

Life for an Eagle. 28

Glossary. 30

Find Out More 31

Index 32

Introducing Eagles

There are many different types of eagle in the world. These amazing **birds of prey** are skilled and deadly hunters. But they are also beautiful creatures, soaring far above the ground.

bald eagle

Harpy eagles are among the largest eagles in the world.

harpy eagle

Where Do Eagles Live?

Eagles live all over the world except in the **continent** of Antarctica. They live wherever there are high places for them to build their nests and there is **prey** for them to hunt.

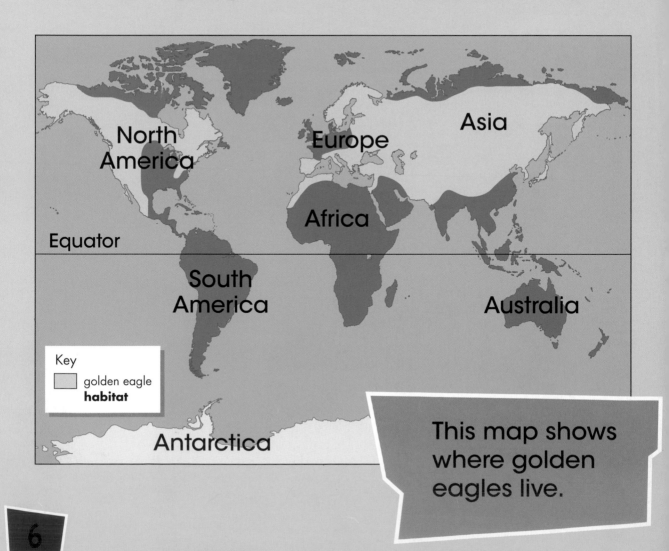

North America

Europe

Asia

Equator

Africa

South America

Australia

Key
golden eagle **habitat**

Antarctica

This map shows where golden eagles live.

Most golden eagles live in California.

What Do Eagles Look Like?

All eagles have feathers on their heads and bodies. Bald eagles are not bald at all. They have white feathers on their heads.

bald eagle

Wings and Tails

All eagles have long, wide wings and a large, fan-shaped tail. Their wings allow them to **glide** for long distances. Eagles can bend the tips of their wings to help them steer. They also move their tails to change direction and to fly higher or lower.

golden eagle

Eagles' long wing feathers are stiff and shaped so the air moves over the wing smoothly.

Bonelli's eagle

11

Beaks and Talons

Eagles have very large, strong beaks. They are hooked and sharp, so they are a perfect tool for ripping **prey** to pieces. Eagles also have sharp, curved **talons**.

golden eagle

beak

Harpy eagles have huge talons. They use them to catch larger prey, such as monkeys.

talon

13

Hunting

Different types of eagle hunt different **prey**. Many eagles, such as golden eagles and wedge-tailed eagles, **glide** high above ground looking for birds and small **mammals**.

Golden eagles mainly hunt rabbits, hares, and other small mammals.

Sea eagles fly over water and snatch up fish in their **talons**.

15

Different Skills

Eagles hunt in different ways. Golden eagles **glide** over open ground before diving down to catch **prey**. Philippine eagles snatch up prey such as monkeys from the branches in forests.

Serpent eagles hunt on the forest floor, where they stab prey with their **talons**.

Philippine eagle

17

Excellent Eyesight

Eagles' large eyes can see **prey** below them from as far as half a mile away. Eagles have two types of vision. They can see in front of them, the way humans do. They can also see out to the sides.

golden eagle

Did you know?
Unlike many animals, eagles can see in color.

bald eagle

Diving

When a golden eagle spots **prey**, it starts to dive to the ground very quickly. It can dive at 150 miles per hour. Eagles often tuck in their wings when they dive, to make them more **streamlined**.

Did you know?
Golden eagles often hunt in pairs, with one chasing prey and the other swooping in to kill.

21

Partners

Golden eagles live in pairs, with one male and one female eagle. They stay together for many years, sometimes all their lives. Each pair of golden eagles has its own **territory**. This is an area of land that provides the food they need.

Did you know?

A golden eagle's territory can be as big as 60 square miles.

Aeries

Pairs of golden eagles make their huge nests together in very high places. An eagle's nest is called an aerie. Eagles build their aeries out of sticks and leaves. They often use the same nest for several years.

Golden eagles build nests in trees, on cliffs, or even on telephone poles.

bald eagle aerie

Eggs and Eaglets

Eagles lay between one and four eggs at a time. The parents take turns sitting on the eggs and keeping them warm. Baby eagles are called eaglets. They are covered in soft **down** when they hatch.

golden eagle

The parents sit on their eggs for around 45 days.

Eaglets are fed by their parents until they are old enough to hunt.

golden eagle

27

Life for an Eagle

Eagles are among the most majestic birds in the sky. It is important that humans protect these beautiful birds and their **habitats,** so that they do not die out.

golden eagle

Did you know?

Eagles can live for up to 30 years.

golden eagle

Glossary

bird of prey bird that hunts and kills birds and other animals for food

continent large land mass, such as Asia, Europe, or Antarctica

crest feathers sticking up on a bird's head

down first, soft feathers on a baby bird

glide move smoothly

habitat natural home for an animal or plant

mammal hair-covered animal that feeds its young on milk

prey animal hunted by another animal for food

streamlined shaped to move easily through air or water

talon bird of prey's claw

territory area of land where one animal or group of animals lives

Find Out More

Books

Magby, Meryl. *Bald Eagles* (American Animals).
New York: PowerKids, 2012.

Morgan, Sally. *Eagles* (Amazing Animal Hunters).
Mankato, Minn.: Amicus, 2011.

Read, Tracy C. *Exploring the World of Eagles.*
Buffalo, N.Y. : Firefly, 2010.

Web sites

Facthound offers a safe, fun way to find web sites related to this book. All the sites on Facthound have been researched by our staff.

Here's all you do:
Visit **www.facthound.com**
Type in this code: 9781410952202

Index

aeries 24, 25

bald eagles 4, 8, 19, 25
beaks 12
birds of prey 4, 30

crests 9, 30

diving 16, 20
down 26, 30

eaglets 26–27
eggs 26
eyesight 18–19

feathers 8, 11

gliding 10, 14, 16, 30
golden eagles 7, 8, 10,
    11, 12, 14, 16, 18, 20, 21,
    22–24, 26, 27, 28-29

habitats 6–7, 28, 30
harpy eagles 5, 13
hawk eagles 9
hunting 6, 16, 21, 27, 28

largest eagles 5
lifespan 29

mammals 14, 30

nests 6, 24, 25

pairs 21, 22–23, 24
Philippine eagles 16, 17
prey 6, 12, 13, 14–15, 16,
    18, 20, 21, 28, 30

sea eagles 15
serpent eagles 16
streamlined shape 20, 30

tails 10

wings 10, 11, 20